CAMBRIDGE ENGLISH
A course for First Certificate

GW00889716

KEY

Margaret Archer
Enid Nolan-Woods

For the Revised Edition

Nelson

Unit one: Housing problems

Dialogue
Exercise
1 They're in a pretty bad condition.
2 Because there's a housing shortage.
3 Some of them haven't got a bathroom or inside toilet.
4 They've been on the housing list since the war.
5 They send a printed postcard saying the matter is receiving attention.
6 She's getting up a petition.
7 She's been asking for volunteers for a protest march.
8 Because he/they/the Moons don't live in Salt Lane.
9 She doesn't know if she's lit her cooker properly.
10 That his firm are/is moving their offices/to Salt Lane next year.

Making Protests
Exercise
1 It's a disgrace
2 It's an absolute scandal
3 It's a shame
4 It's not right
5 It's all wrong
6 It's not fair

N.B. Variations are possible in the protests used for each statement, the order is
not rigid; but one of each type should be employed.

Listening and Choosing
Text 1
1 *B* 2 *B* 3 *B* 4 *A*

Text 2
1 John Green 40
   17 Park Avenue, Hendon
   781 2459
   Accountant
   Benson and Black, Churchill House, Hendon
   Six years
   House
   Three
   Garden, garage
   £55,000

2 *C* 3 *C* 4 *A* 5 *C*

Look and Learn
1 Classic/Grecian design; elegant houses with statues, columns, etc.
2 For decoration, to add importance, because of the neo-classic style.
3 Free answer.
4 To support the porch; for decoration.

Reading Aloud
1 A student accommodation officer.
2 Rent and living expenses are less; there's not much chance of being lonely.
3 To agree certain things first, such as who will see that rent and bills are paid;
   how much will each person contribute; will people buy their own food and d▮

their own cooking; what arrangements will be made about cleaning, washing up and entertaining friends.

N.B.   Answers may vary, but should include the points given above.

Structures: Exercises   Reading/Writing   A/B

Exercise 1

1 have been waiting
2 is (always) digging
3 Have / haven't decided / agreed / planned / managed
4 build / are building
5 has (just) read / checked / is (just) reading / checking
6 are moving / move
7 aren't
8 has / hasn't made / published / agreed / passed / proclaimed
9 Is . . . coming / calling?
10 meets
11 are going
12 have been trying
13 Is / Isn't?
14 Has (never) lived
15 are building / constructing
16 have been saving / looking / waiting / hoping
17 see / understand . . . are moving
18 have (already) moved
19 Do . . . know?
20 hasn't had / received

Exercise 2

1 Is . . . doing?
2 believe . . is mowing
3 haven't been sleeping
4 is
5 have been trying
6 are . . . painting
7 is not / isn't
8 has finished
9 Have . . . seen?
10 is

Exercise 3

The following are suggestions for completion of the sentences. There are variations of course, which will occur to students and teachers.

1 is garish / bizarre / too bright
2 has been designing new schools / houses / buildings, etc.
3 never stop playing loud music / are always singing / shouting, etc.
4 are still empty / have never been occupied
5 has been trying to control / has controlled rents
6 stop work / working / go home / leave work
7 have already stopped / gone
8 owns / have built all of / some of / most of the houses
9 like living here / have lived here all my life
10 are owned by me / my wife, etc. / are kept in the bank

Vocabulary: Photograph   Reading/Writing   C

Exercise

1 detached
2 tiles / slates
3 gutter / drainpipe
4 down the drainpipe / down the drain
5 chimney stack
6 a pane
7 shutters
8 window sill
9 attic
10 cellar / basement
11 frame
12 porch
13 knocker
14 chains
15 letter box
16 aerial
17 fence
18 gate
19 garage / port
20 dustbin

Asking Questions   Reading/Writing   D

Exercise 1

1 Why has Esmeralda Hotchkiss written to / consulted the estate agent?
2 How many bedrooms does she / Ms Hotchkiss / Esmeralda want?

3 Where does Tiger / the cat like to sit?
4 How does Tiger / the cat get in at night?
5 Where does Tiger / the cat sleep during the winter?
6 Has Polly ever been kept in a cage?
7 What kind / type of windows does Polly prefer?
8 How does Polly turn the hot water tap on and off?
9 Why must there be a fitted carpet in Polly's room?
10 What makes Polly very irritable / use bad language?
11 Who has asked Esmeralda Hotchkiss to find other accommodation as soon as possible?
12 Who have the neighbours upstairs / in the flat above / been complaining about?

Exercise 2

1 Is there a fitted kitchen?
2 How many bedrooms are there?
3 How much / What is the rent?
4 Is there central heating?
5 Is there plenty of storage space / How much storage space is there?
6 What are / How much are the rates?
7 Are there any built-in wardrobes?
8 What's the telephone number?
9 What size / How big is the sitting room?
10 When can I move in?
11 Who is the owner / Who does the flat belong to?
12 Is there a lift?

Exercise 3

The following letter can be used as a guide. There are many variations, but students should use all of the information given in the text.

Dear Mr Hodge,

   I should like to make a few inquiries about the house you have for sale.

   Firstly, could you tell me where the house is situated and how far it is from the station?

   Secondly, perhaps you could tell me what type of house it is and if it has a garden? I should, of course, like to know what the accommodation consists of; how many bedrooms and reception rooms it contains. Is there central heating, and if so, what type? Is the kitchen fitted with cupboards, and is there plenty of storage space?

   I assume that there is a garage, but if not, where can I park my car?

   I'm sorry to trouble you with all these questions but before considering buying I naturally need to know if the accommodation is what I require. I should appreciate it if I could come and look at the house some time, if it doesn't inconvenience you.

> Thanking you in advance for your help,
> Yours sincerely,
> Joan Stevens (Mrs)

Making Complaints   Reading/Writing   E

Exercise 1

The following are suggestions for completing the complaints. There are variations which will occur to students and teachers, but in each case a form of complaint should be used and the verbs should be in one of the Present Tenses.

1 I'm writing to complain about my electric wiring which is faulty and therefore extremely dangerous.
2 When do you intend to do something about my gas cooker? I have been awaiting delivery for six months and I have no other means of cooking.

3 I've been complaining about dry rot in my dining room floor boards ever since I moved in. Would you please do something about it, as it's impossible to lay a carpet.

4 I'm extremely annoyed about my electricity bill which I consider excessive as I use only one small fire in the back bedroom.

5 Why haven't you done something about the lighting on the stairs? It is quite inadequate and extremely unsafe for the residents.

6 How many times do I have to tell you about my leaking roof? It is badly damaging my bedroom carpet and ruining the furniture.

7 I'm writing to complain about my cold water tank. It gurgles at night and disturbs my sleep.

8 When do you intend to do something about the broken window in my kitchen? It's an open invitation to burglars.

9 I'm extremely annoyed about the recent rent increase as I feel it's completely unjustified.

10 Why haven't you done something about the outside paintwork? It's peeling dreadfully and looks an absolute disgrace, especially as this is a good neighbourhood.

Exercise 2

The residents have been complaining for a year about the dangerous stairs in our block.

We want to know why you haven't done anything about it yet.

As the landlord you are responsible for repairs.

These stairs are particularly dangerous for old people at night.

When do you intend to do something about it?

Exercise 3

1 I'm writing to complain again about the central heating at the Midas Rest Home.

2 It is much too cold in the sitting-room and the television room so the old people wear overcoats.

3 The faulty ventilation system causes draughts in nearly all the rooms.

4 There are worn-out radiators upstairs which give / are giving little warmth in the bedrooms.

5 The bathroom heater hasn't worked / been working for six months.

6 The residents have been complaining / have complained all winter but no one appears to care.

7 It is a scandal particularly in view of the fees that the residents pay.

8 When do you intend to do something about it?

9 Everyone visiting / who visits the Home says it is a disgrace.

10 I propose to take up the matter with the Council if you do not take action immediately.

Unit two: Traffic problems

Dialogue   Oral **A**

Exercise

1 ... he wasn't looking where he was going.

2 Because she had the right of way.

3 She noticed that the man driver was driving much too fast.

4 Because he'd just looked at his speedometer.

5 The bumper was dented, one of the headlights was broken, and the bonnet was scratched.

6 Because she had been talking a lot / so much.
7 It had just been serviced.
8 ... the man's fault.
9 Because he drove over a crossroads without looking.
10 The woman had jumped the traffic lights / crossed the traffic lights when they were red.

Making Apologies   Oral B

Exercise
a 1–8: Any of the forms of apology with *for*
b 1–8: Any of the other forms of apology.

Look and Talk   Oral C

Questions
1 The scene shows a three-lane motorway, with traffic travelling in both directions and slip roads on the left and right.
2 It's a slip road to allow traffic to leave the motorway and take the A2203 to Greenwich. Further along another slip road allows traffic to enter the motorway.
3 The metal barrier is to prevent traffic crossing the centre reservation.
4 It is probably going to try to overtake the first lorry.
5 The inside lane is for slow-moving traffic, the centre lane is for driving along at normal speed, the outside lane is for overtaking.

Reading Aloud   Oral D

1 It refers to some of the many anti-theft devices available which can prevent cars being stolen.
2 It advises using either a hook and rod-type device, a handbrake lock, a secret switch to cut out the ignition or a device connected to the car horn.
3 The police, a newspaper or magazine article, a radio or television programme, a shop selling anti-theft devices, etc.

Structures: Exercises   Reading/Writing A/B

Exercise

1 drove / went
2 was
3 was riding
4 did he have
5 was (always) getting
6 broke down
7 did you manage
8 had removed / had towed away
9 looked
10 was running
11 was turning / turned / reached
12 drove
13 had forgotten
14 had been driving
15 changed / went green
16 wasn't looking
17 had phoned
18 had been trying
19 hadn't had
20 were
21 lost
22 were waiting
23 was driving
24 Didn't you see
25 cleaned / wiped / was cleaning / was wiping ... put / was putting
26 had indicated / had signalled
27 wasn't driving
28 pulled in
29 were stopping / checking / inspecting
30 were driving / going.

Vocabulary Reading/Writing **C**

Reading comprehension

1 *D* 2 *C* 3 *D* 4 *C* 5 *A* 6 *D* 7 *C* 8 *B* 9 *A* 10 *C* 11 *A* 12 *D* 13 *C*
14 *B* 15 *D* 16 *C* 17 *B* 18 *D* 19 *A* 20 *A*

Ask and Answer Reading/Writing **D**

1 When did the little girl step out into the road? When the lorry began to accelerate.
2 She was leading a very large dog.
3 How did the lorry driver brake? He braked as hard as he could.
4 Because he stopped with such a jerk.
5 He felt irate / angry.
6 What were the little girl and the dog doing? They were proceeding calmly across the road.
7 Because she wasn't looking where she was going.
8 … she was thinking of something else.
9 What was the dog doing? Taking the little girl for a walk.
10 What had the little girl promised to buy? She'd promised to buy two tins of baked beans.
11 Because she'd been so busy looking at things in the market.
12 … she'd spent all the money her mother had given her.
13 What did the dog do while the conversation was going on? He managed to detach himself from the lead.
14 Where did the dog go? He went round to the back of the lorry.
15 Because he was large and very strong.
16 What happened when he did? All the contents spilled on to the road.
17 … he saw what he had done.
18 He wagged his tail.
19 She thought he was very clever.
20 What hadn't the dog forgotten? He hadn't forgotten the baked beans.

Making Excuses Reading/Writing **E**

Exercise 1

Son I couldn't help it, I was trying to put it away in the garage.

As I was backing the car in, the wind blew the door shut; it wasn't my fault.

I'm sorry, I was only trying to help.

I'm sorry I scratched / damaged it, I didn't mean to.

Exercise 2

1 I couldn't help it, my brakes failed.
2 I didn't mean to leave my keys in the car.
3 I was only trying to help you.
4 It wasn't my fault my car was stolen.

How to extract information Reading/Writing **F**

Exercise 1

1 If he drives for a long time without adequate periods of rest; if he keeps a steady speed for a long time; if his car is not adequately ventilated; if warmth and cigarette fumes create a fug and cause a lack of oxygen; if his seat position needs adjusting.
2 Cigarette fumes, especially when combined with warmth in winter from the car heater, can create a fug; this causes a lack of oxygen and can make the driver feel drowsy.

3 Stop and rest at the first sign of fatigue; stretch, take some breaths of fresh air, and walk about; make sure the car has adequate ventilation; drive with the window slightly open; make sure the airflow is working properly; boost the air supply occasionally; vary the driving speed; adjust the seat position; have head or backrests fitted if necessary; don't drink and drive.

Exercise 2
1 Patricia Adams. She needs a powerful car for her frequent business trips and country weekends; she is single, so she doesn't need a car with a lot of space either for passengers or luggage; her car must be smart-looking to suit her expensive life-style.
2 ... such as its ability to travel at high speed, its unconventional style and its high price, it is not likely that Helen Williamson would buy it; she needs a car mainly for leisure use and occasional business trips; she prefers a four-door car.
3 Jonny Le Beau. Its lack of interior space; he needs a car that can carry several people; however, he would like all the other features, such as its appearance, speed and reliability.

Exercise 3
1 ... a fall in the total number of accidents, from 267,528 to 246,370, a drop of over 21,000; there was also a fall in the total number of casualties, the greatest decrease being in the number of people seriously injured.
2 ... fell between 1967 and 1982, the greatest decrease being between 1967 and 1972; between 1972 and 1977 the total number of accidents remained almost constant, but in 1977 there were over 12,000 fewer injuries than in 1972.
3 ... will show a fall in both the number of accidents and of casualties; the number of people killed may not be much less than in 1982, but the number of seriously injured may be a lot less, and the number of slightly injured may be slightly less.

N.B. In the above three exercises, answers will vary, but should include the points given.

Unit three: Amusements
Dialogue   Oral A
Exercise
1 Who will be opening the fair?
2 He hopes she'll be wearing more clothes than she was in *Shoot the Lady*.
3 What is the theme of the fair going to be? 'Britain through the Ages'.
4 They'll be wearing period costumes / clothes.
5 How many Union Jacks will the children have made by the end of the week?
6 What sort of amusements will there be? There will be hoop-la, a coconut shy and all sorts of competitions.
7 He's going to raffle a pig.
8 He'll be able to show Stephen that he is better at shooting than him / than he is.
9 What will Stephen have done before the date of the fair? He'll have managed to lift twice his own weight.
10 Because she'll need him to move a couple of heavy tables down from the attic / Because there'll be a lot to do.
11 They won't be able to put the refreshment tent up.
12 Where will Peter be on Saturday?
13 How much is Peter going to send Lucy? He's going to send her £10.

14 He'll be thinking of her.
15 Because he'll say anything to get out of doing any hard work.

Making and Accepting Invitations

Exercise 1
1 Why don't we go to the fair?
2 How about going to the seaside?
3 What about going to the country?
4 Let's go to a pop concert.
5 I wonder if you'd like to go to the circus?
6 Would you be able to go to the zoo?
7 Would you like to go to an Art Gallery?
8 Would it interest you to go to a football match?

Exercise 2
Free choice of invitations; students should try to use all of them.

N.B.   *Let's* cannot be used with the verb *come*.

Exercise 3
1 I'd like to very much.
2 Thank you very much.
3 I'd love to.
4 That'd be very nice.
5 Yes, let's.
6 I'd love to.
7 That's very kind of you.
8 That's a good idea.

Variations are possible in some of the phrases of acceptance used; the student should try to use all of the phrases.

Listening Comprehension

1   Dick Sharp   Andy Norman   Steve Robson   Geoff Burns

2 *B*   **3** *C*   **4** *B*

Reading Aloud

1 At a Sports Club.
2 A membership form and a leaflet.
3 Fill in the form, and look at the leaflet and choose which sports he wants to take part in.
4 The subscription to the Club has to be paid in advance.

Look and Say

1 They are listening to a fairground organ.
2 Probably jolly, cheerful tunes – possibly from Holland.
3 It's an organ built into the back of a truck, very decorative with small figures of musicians playing instruments at the front. It's Dutch as it comes from Amsterdam.
4 It's probably in a park as part of a festival, or maybe just to provide entertainment for the public at the weekend.

Structures: Exercises

Exercise 1
1 shall / will / 'll (never) be able.
2 Are you going
3 will have been talking
4 will not / won't be finished / over
5 is / 's playing
6 will you be
7 shall / will / 'll meet / see / wait for
8 Isn't
9 will be appearing / playing / performing
10 will have reached / got to
11 Will (he) have got / reached
12 are going to hear
13 will have been travelling / driving

14 will it take	**18** they will give / they'll give
15 will / 'll tell / am / 'm going to tell	**19** will finish / end
16 are going	**20** is going / will be going
17 isn't coming / won't come / won't be coming	

Exercise 2

1 isn't going to / won't start / begin	**6** (he)'ll see
2 will (the musicians) receive	**7** will (all) be gone
3 will have been singing	**8** will (the show) be over
4 Are (you) going to bring	**9** will have made
5 won't be coming (as he)'s going	**10** (I)'ll / shall / will never forget

Exercise 3

1 She'll have to decide where to go for her holiday.
2 The advertisements, brochures and special offers will start dropping through her letter box.
3 Trying their hardest; making an effort; doing their utmost.
4 She will improve her physique.
5 She will have learnt something new / increased her knowledge.
6 Because a wide variety of things / most things can be studied there.
7 She's afraid she'll become too distracted to choose.
8 She won't be able to afford to go on holiday unless she gets a rise.

Exercise 4

1 The circus tent.	**6** By laughing / talking / eating sweets etc.
2 On the village green.	**7** Somersaults, cartwheels, balancing acts.
3 It won't be big / deep enough.	**8** They will fall into the net.
4 They constantly move from place to place / They never remain in one place for long.	**9** They do all the things we'd love to do but never dare do.
5 not to mention / as well as.	**10** Contented, happy, satisfied.

Ask and Answer   Reading/Writing C

1 What is the man with the little boy doing? He's teaching the little boy to turn somersaults / to do acrobatics.
2 He'll roll over / stand up.
3 Why is the man wearing stockings? Because it protects his legs / keeps his legs warm / is part of the costume for the fair.
4 He's going to try to do / turn a somersault.
5 The boy will have finished turning a somersault.
6 Where is this taking place? It's taking place outdoors / in a park / on the common as part of the fair.
7 How long will it take to become a good acrobat? It will take several years / a very long time.
8 No, probably not. Yes, they possibly will. No, they probably won't.
9 What will the children be doing in half an hour's time? They'll be turning somersaults / still learning how to turn somersaults / they'll be going home.
10 I think this man will have been working for X hours / for a very long time.

Using Links and Joins   Reading/Writing D

Exercise 1

1 who	**3** where / because / as	**5** as soon as
2 but	**4** so that	**6** where / as

7	although	11	unless	14	if
8	but	12	after	15	but / even though /
9	therefore / so	13	because		although
10	while				

Exercise 2

1	doesn't expect to pass.	8	they sell cheap fruit and
2	I protested.		vegetables.
3	she forgot to buy his cigarettes.	9	he can borrow his father's car.
4	we can dance.	10	you know the result.
5	I was ill on the boat.	11	going on to Oxford.
6	her brother has a music lesson.	12	they come back from holiday.
7	she's gone to the doctor's for a	13	hearing from the bank.
	check up.	14	there is no restaurant car.

N.B.   The above completions are only suggestions. Teachers and students will, no doubt, think of many variations of their own.

Exercise 3

1	that	8	until	15	where
2	when / after	9	because	16	and
3	and	10	if	17	even though
4	since	11	and / or	18	when / after
5	when	12	then	19	although
6	while	13	but	20	so
7	so that	14	therefore / so		

Exercise 4

1	although	3	even though	5	and
2	so	4	so that	6	when

Refusing Invitations   Reading/Writing   **E**

Exercise 1

1	It's very kind of you but I don't really like the ballet.	4	I'm sorry, I can't manage it.
2	I'm afraid I'm not free on Saturday.	5	I'm afraid I can't.
3	I'm sorry, I'm already booked up on Sunday.	6	I'm so sorry, I'm busy.

Exercise 2

1–9: various combinations of invitations and refusals are possible.

Exercise 3

Jane   I'm sorry, I can't manage it as it's my Drama Club night.
I'm so sorry, I'm busy baby-sitting for Mrs Harris.
I'm afraid I can't as I saw it last week with Charles.
I'm afraid I'm not free as I have to work late.
It's very kind of you but I don't really like Brighton.
I'm sorry, I'm already booked up.

N.B.   Variations of refusals are permissible.

Unit four: Education

Dialogue   Oral   **A**

Exercise 1

1   They feel he ought to take up something more secure than art.
2   There'd be no guarantee he'd get a good job afterwards.

3   He suggests William could teach.
4   He says he wouldn't be a teacher if it were the last job on earth.
5   The Headmaster would have liked to be an actor.
6   Because the entry qualifications wouldn't be so stiff.
7   He'd have to do a year's foundation course first.
8   He'd get a grant provided he'd got the right 'O's' and 'A's'.
9   He'd better accept the fact that nowadays young people don't worry about security.
10 Because he could find out about William's chances of being accepted at Art School.
11 To let him know what Mr Sims (the Art Master) says.
12 He'll be all right so long as he does as well as he's doing at present.

Exercise 2

The following are suggested answers to the questions, but any alternative answer formed with the Simple Future Tense is allowable.

1   I'll be late for work / school / college.
2   I'll go to the seaside / country / mountains.
3   I'll buy some new clothes / put it in the bank.
4   I'll ask somebody.
5   I'll tell the ticket collector / inspector.
6   I'll call the doctor / I'll go to hospital.

Exercise 3

Any answer formed with the 'would' Conditional is permissible. The following are only suggested answers.

1   I'd get up and investigate / I'd put my head under the pillow.
2   I'd take it to the police station.
3   I'd break a window / I'd borrow a ladder.
4   I'd ask someone to translate / I'd go to a class and learn English.
5   I'd inform the police / I'd go to the police station.
6   I'd put it out / I'd find out what it was.

Exercise 4

Any answer formed with the 'would have' Conditional is permissible. The following are suggested answers.

1   I would have told the waiter.
2   I'd have offered to have it repaired.
3   I'd have cleaned it off / I'd have wiped it up.
4   I'd have apologised / I'd have gone home again.
5   I'd have bought her a present the next day / I'd have taken her out.
6   I'd have mended it / I'd have bought a new one.

Giving Advice   Oral B

Exercise

A variety of answers are possible, but the student should be careful to use one of the forms of advice learnt.

1   If I were you I'd go to the doctor's.
2   I think you ought to see a dentist.
3   You'd better go to the police station.
4   It would be a good idea if you sat it again.
5   You'd better not argue with the police.
6   I think the best thing would be to go to a good English school.
7   You'd better go to an optician immediately.

8 I think you ought to apologise.

9 It would be a good idea if you offered to have it mended.

10 If I were you I'd get up earlier.

Look and Explain

Oral   **C**

1 Any reasonable description allowable.

2 To stop the children from running out into the road and perhaps having an accident.

3 Yes – quiet, pleasant surroundings in the country, probably small classes, family atmosphere. No – too small, not enough equipment – too quiet, no city stimulation – possibly closed atmosphere.

4 Built in old days when coal fires were used; possibly they still are.

Listening Comprehension

Oral   **D**

	MONDAY	TUESDAY	WEDNESDAY	THURSDAY	FRIDAY
9.30 to 10.45	Review of week's work *Intensive text study*	Dialogue work (idiomatic spoken English)	Intensive text study	*Dialogue work (intonation)*	*Recall – Test on all items learnt during week*
11.00 to 12.00	Grammar practice (remedial work and new items) *Pronunciation*	*Extensive reading* Pronunciation	*News broadcast (study of the day's news)*	*Grammar (phrasal verb review)* *Spelling practice*	Roleplay/ Simulation or Project work
12.05 to 13.00	Listening comprehension (Group and pair work – often in Listening Centre)	*Activity period (reading task homework)*	Dictionary work – Individual work in library or Listening Centre	*Listening and discussion*	*Free oral activity work*

Reading Aloud

Oral   **E**

1 In a school

2 The head teacher

3 Not to push or shove, and not to run or shout.

Communication Exercise

Oral   **F**

Anna buys a pencil and a notebook. As Juan doesn't buy either a pen or a notebook, he must therefore buy two pencils. As Anna doesn't buy a pen, she must therefore buy the pencil and notebook.

Structures: Exercises

Reading/Writing   **A/B**

Exercise 1

1 were – wouldn't go

2 should / would be – could / would give

3 had known – would have met (you) / picked (you) up

4 wouldn't have gone – had rained

5 would (you) do / would (you) have done – closed / had been closed

6 hadn't spent – would be

7 was wondering / wonder – could help / would help

8 failed / had failed / fail – would sit / take / do, would have sat / taken / done will sit / take / do

9 should / would be   should / would have been   shall / will be – let – go

10 wouldn't have learnt / known – had not / hadn't gone

11 go – wake up

12 practise – won't speak

13 wouldn't have noticed / seen – hadn't waved

14 Will / won't – is closed / shut

15 had been – would / could / might have been burnt

16 won't go, wouldn't have gone – receives / gets, had received / got

17 will get better / will be all right – take

18 keep / had kept – will be / would have been

19 would like

20 Will (you) buy – pay

Exercise 2

1 attended / had attended – would learn / would have learnt

2 Will you go / Are you going – pass

3 were / had been – would study / would have studied

4 would have won – had tried

5 sit – will tell

6 will happen / would happen – closes / closed

7 will never speak – doesn't study

8 would stop – could concentrate

9 will it take / would it take – go / went

10 is – won't

Exercise 3

Free choice of completion; student should be careful to use the correct Conditional form.

Exercise 4

1 were	**9** wouldn't be	**17** had had
2 wouldn't waste	**10** said / were to say	**18** would have done
3 wouldn't be	**11** would be	**19** had made
4 would spend	**12** would be	**20** would have been
5 had had	**13** might be	**21** would find
6 had known	**14** could have sprung	**22** were
7 could have understood	**15** wouldn't have been able	**23** wants
8 were	**16** hadn't been	**24** would be

Ask and Answer   Reading/Writing   **C**

1 How old is this college?

2 What is unusual about the big window over the door? It has a rose / flower motif at the top.

3 For ornament / decoration.

4 What is the purpose of the monument in front of the college?

5 What would the effect be if there were no trees round the college? It would look very bare / bleak.

6 … would look very plain.

7 … of the spire on the roof / of the big window above the door.

8 Where do the students study?

9 How much does it cost to go to this college? Probably a lot of money.

10 What would happen if this college were built near a main road? It would be very noisy / dirty.

Information Retrieval

1 Maria Rossi. She has been in Bath less than a year, so is not likely to know it or its surroundings very well; she is interested in British culture and customs; she could probably afford it as her father sends her money.
2 Hans Schmitt. He already knows about some aspects of British art and culture and the course would introduce him to others; since his present course finishes in July, he is not likely to be studying or working during August.
3 Jose Gomez may not be interested; his parents are visiting him at the time the course is being held.
4 Barbara Green; as she doesn't have much money she probably wouldn't be able to afford the course; in any case, she needs to work during the vacation to supplement her grant.

N.B.   The answers will vary, but should include the points given above.

Using should – would – could

Exercise 1

1	should	5	shouldn't	8	would
2	couldn't	6	could	9	would / could
3	'd rather	7	wouldn't / shouldn't	10	wouldn't
4	would				

Exercise 2

1 couldn't see where we were going
2 should see a doctor.
3 would always drink a pint of beer each day.
4 should go on a diet.
5 I would rather go by car.
6 would look better in a silver frame.
7 I'd rather not go to the concert tonight.
8 would / could have met you.
9 we couldn't take any photographs / pictures.
10 I'd rather not see it.

The above are suggested completions of the sentences. Many variations are possible but the student should be careful to use the right form *should*, *would*, *could* or *would rather*.

Exercise 3

1 He would have bought a large estate and stocked it with deer and other wild animals.
2 He could double it.
3 Because he couldn't imagine having a lot of money.
4 He swept and dusted the cottage and cooked the supper.
5 They said he would rather waste his time at the cottage than do an honest day's work.
6 He would soon have been in trouble.
7 She was surprised at his concern for her.
8 ... wouldn't have got very far.
9 ... it couldn't have come from the same tree as the red ones.
10 Because she thought he couldn't find another one strong enough to carry half the apples.
11 He wished he could do a trick like that.
12 Because he hadn't asked the old woman indoors.
13 He wondered if it would produce apples of pure gold if he planted it.
14 He thought Silly could have dreamt the whole story.
15 It was real / He hadn't dreamt it.

Exercise 4

1 was once.
2 Because the boy in the photo didn't have a beard.
3 would have been if the circumstances had been different.
4 Their parents would get into trouble.
5 ... they broke a window.
6 It was very silly and wrong.
7 Always being good and correct isn't very exciting.
8 She thought he would have a bad influence on the children.
9 He would begin to laugh.
10 They didn't speak to each other for a week.

What to do and how to do it   Reading/Writing F

What to do on your first day at a new school

School begins at 9 a.m. when you should assemble in the school hall. Then at 9.15 you should report to your class teacher for a timetable. After that at 9.30 go to the library prepared to take a general knowledge test which lasts until 10.30, when the new pupils will be given a medical inspection. From 11 a.m. to 11.15 there is a break for milk and biscuits in the school hall. The normal timetable then continues until 12.45, when there is a lunchbreak in the school dining room in the annexe, until 2 o'clock. After lunch school continues with the normal timetable until 4 p.m.

Tuesday and Wednesday afternoons are given over to football and basketball respectively. All information about school clubs and activities is displayed on the notice board in the hall. You should wear the school uniform at all times and you are not allowed to smoke or eat in the classroom or talk in the corridors.

Exercise 1

Mr Robinson will have to catch the 8.36 train from Liverpool Street Station arriving at Hamford at 9.45 in time for his meeting at 10.30. To get to Barminster by 1 o'clock in time for lunch, he will have to catch the 12.26 from Hamford, arriving at Barminster at 12.43. Then to arrive back in London by 6 p.m. he will have to catch the 16.43 from Barminster arriving at Liverpool Street Station at 17.42.

Exercise 2

To look up a number in a London telephone directory first select the correct volume. Remember all surnames are listed alphabetically; the initials, also in alphabetic order, follow the surname. Check that you have the correct spelling for the name. The address follows the initials, and the phone number comes last on the right hand side of the page. The phone number will start with 01, the code number for London (which should not be dialled if you are already in London), followed by seven figures. The first 3 figures are the district code, followed by 4 figures which are the subscriber's personal number. Dial all seven figures. If the telephone number is not listed in the directory check with Directory Enquiries as the number may be ex-directory.

Unit five: Holidays and water sports

Drills and Comprehension   Oral B

Exercise (Gerunds)

1 Sitting around and doing nothing.
2 He enjoys swimming and water skiing.
3 He doesn't mind roughing it.

16

4 He's been used to looking after himself.
5 It includes one week's skin-diving and one week's shark-fishing.
6 He doesn't fancy shark-fishing.
7 If there's any chance of sailing.
8 If he's interested in rowing.
9 He did a lot of rowing.
10 He suggests Mr Hope tries riding.
11 He remembers him saying he wanted an active holiday.
12 He's never done any riding.
13 He doesn't want to do a lot of travelling.
14 If he would mind letting him have some brochures and leaflets.
15 He's going to enjoy looking at them.

Exercise

What do you like doing on Sundays?

Have you ever done any fishing?

Would you like to come swimming?

Where would you go to learn water-skiing?

5 What would you wear for skin-diving?

6 Are you any good at rowing?

7 Have you ever tried playing golf?

8 Why do you like sunbathing?

Exercise

1 Where do you like going at the week-end?
2 Have you ever been shark-fishing?
3 Would you like to try canoeing?
4 Where would you go to watch water-skiing?
5 Have you ever tried playing tennis?
6 Which do you like better, swimming or sunbathing?
7 What would you wear for rowing?
8 Do you remember learning to swim?
9 Do you enjoy playing golf?
10 Where are you thinking of spending your holidays?

Exercise (Infinitives)

1 Holidays to suit individual tastes / needs.
2 To make sure your holiday is a success.
3 ... to do something more energetic.
4 ... to please.

5 To assist you in every way they can.
6 To book early.
7 ... to worry.
8 If you wish to alter your booking.
9 To make a small extra charge.
10 ... make changes of timetable.

Asking for Information   Oral   C

Exercise

One Excuse me, can / could you tell me the times of the trains to Brighton, please?
How long does it take to get there / to Brighton?
Is there a restaurant car on the train?
Do you know if there is a sailing school at Brighton? /
Is there a sailing school at Brighton?

Reading Aloud   Oral   D

It is about booking a holiday.
In a travel agency.

3 When people have decided which holiday they want, they must pay £25 to secure a booking.

4 By cash, cheque or credit card.

Look and Understand

Photograph

1 They are cleaning / painting / mending the boat.

2 It's cheap / romantic / compact. You can move around, explore the rivers, canals, moor in different places. Gives an illusion of being a sailor.

3 Operating the locks, meeting another boat coming from the opposite direction on a narrow stretch, turning at tight bends.

4 No, not really, except you don't change gear.

Structures: Exercises

Exercise 1

1	rowing / swimming	8	swimming	15	must go / get
2	to go / drive	9	waiting	16	swimming / diving
3	standing (up)	10	to buy / get	17	Diving / Swimming
4	going	11	catch	18	to tell
5	to hear / get / have	12	to have	19	to go / sail
6	try / put	13	eating / buying	20	complain / grumble
7	getting	14	gutting / skinning / cutting up		

Exercise 2

1	rowing	5	crossing	8	phoning
2	see	6	to sit	9	land
3	to pay	7	to phone	10	to spend / fishing
4	Punting				

Exercise 3

The following completions are only suggestions; many more variations are possible, but students should be careful to get a correct Infinitive or Gerund form.

1	to swim in / row on / dive into the lake	6	to stand (up) here
2	ringing	7	waiting for hours for a bite
3	to reach port on time	8	fighting
4	re-spraying / repainting	9	taking it / buying it
5	to cross	10	to rest / to have a rest / to sit dow

Exercise 4

1	to swim	11	to keep	21	to get
2	to laugh	12	to capsize	22	hitting
3	floundering	13	rowing	23	to being
4	splashing	14	running	24	watching
5	getting	15	jumping	25	doing
6	propelling	16	hurdling	26	to congratulate
7	using	17	weight-lifting	27	saying
8	swimming	18	to play	28	saying
9	rowing	19	to appear	29	worrying
10	to manage	20	boxing	30	to see

Exercise 5

1	to hire	3	sailing / fishing	5	mending
2	to pay	4	to tell	6	to know

7	fishing / sailing / boating	9	to make	12	seeing
8	to shout	10	hear	13	know
		11	talking	14	to hire

Vocabulary: Photograph

Reading/Writing **C**

1 Rowing boats.
2 By using oars.
3 Wood.
4 steer
5 drown
6 rough / ruffled
7 tie up; drift
8 By working the rudder.
9 shadows / reflections
10 One is rowing, the other steering the boat.

Reading and Understanding

Reading/Writing **D**

Passage 1
B 2 C 3 C 4 A 5 A

Passage 2
C 2 A 3 B 4 A 5 A

Passage 3

Malaga	Hotel San Carlos	July 23rd	14
Gatwick	Malaga		
1st room	Mr F SIMPSON		
	Mrs S SIMPSON		
2nd room	Mrs A HARVEY		
	Miss M SIMPSON	10	
3rd room	Mr T SIMPSON	11	
	Mr R HARVEY		
	Mr E HARVEY		

Half board
Deposit £175 cheque
B 3 C 4 B

Information Retrieval

Reading/Writing **E**

Britain	D	USA	B
France	E	Greece	C
India	A	Italy	F

1 E 2 A 3 F 4 D 5 B 6 C
World Wide Travel are a travel agency; experienced in sending people on holidays to exotic places; they are holding a competition and will send the winner for a free holiday in America.
By completing three simple questions, anyone has a chance of winning a holiday; the winner will visit New York, Dallas, the Grand Canyon, Las Vegas, Los Angeles, Hollywood and Disneyland.

N.B. The answers will vary, but should include these points.

Unit six: Crime and detection

Drills and Exercises

Oral **B**

1 He'd been to the garage to have his car headlights tested / He'd been having his car headlights tested at the garage.
2 If no one was in, they were always left in a box at the back door.
3 It had been propped up against a / his aunt's bedroom window.

4 It had been broken.

5 The pots had probably been used to break the window / The pieces had fallen inside when the window had been broken.

6 It had been ripped apart / torn open.

7 She would never have any of the lights turned on until necessary / unnecessarily / when they weren't needed.

8 She'd been hit with something / That was where she'd been hit.

9 He suspected his aunt had been murdered.

10 He knew nothing must be touched or moved before / until the police arrived came.

11 The criminal always gets caught.

12 She was loved and respected by everyone / He'd never heard an unkind word spoken about her.

Exercise 3

1 The telephone wire's been cut	**5** The whisky's been spilt
2 The mirror's been smashed	**6** The drawer's been forced open
3 The vase's been broken	**7** The tap's been left on
4 The carpet's been muddied	**8** The television's been turned on

Exercise 4

1 Was it the one she was shot with?

2 Was it the one she was hit with?

3 Was it the one she was smothered with?

4 Were they the ones she was tortured with?

5 Was it the one she was slashed with?

6 Was it the one she was strangled with?

7 Was it the one she was stabbed with?

8 Was it the one she was murdered with?

Expressing Surprise and Dismay   Oral

Exercise 1

1 It was *terrible* / awful / ghastly / appalling!

2 *It was incredible!* / It's quite extraordinary!

3 It's quite extraordinary!

4 It was *appalling* / terrible / *ghastly* / awful!

5 It was terrible / awful / *incredible!*

6 *It's quite extraordinary* / It was incredible!

The students should be encouraged to vary these phrases but the most suitable are in italics.

appalling and *ghastly* are usually used to indicate an extremely shocking or disturbing event.

extraordinary and *incredible* indicate an event that is difficult to believe.

Note Change of tense from 'It was' to 'It's' is permissible; e.g. It's terrible! It's incredible! etc.

Exercise 2

The student should be encouraged to vary his responses from the following:

How awful! How terrible! How ghastly! How appalling! How extraordinary! How incredible!

Listening Comprehension   Oral

1 *A*   2 *G*   3 *J*   4 *C*   5 *D*
6 *F*   7 *I*   8 *B*   9 *H*   10 *E*

Look and Describe   Oral **E**

There is a knife with a sharp blade and a wooden handle; a soft, striped cushion; an axe (or chopper) with a wooden handle and a sharp / keen edge; a small, black gun / revolver; needles of various sizes; some sharp razor blades, and one of them is inserted in a handle like a knife; a hammer with a wooden handle and a heavy steel head; and a nylon stocking.
(N.B.   Answers as exercise 4)
Somebody could: stab someone with a knife, shoot someone with a gun, murder someone with an axe, hit someone with a hammer, strangle someone with a nylon stocking, smother someone with a cushion, torture someone with needles, slash someone with a razor blade.

and **4**   Free answer.

Reading Aloud   Oral **F**

In the Chamber of Horrors (in Madame Tussaud's in London).
The guide.
The wax models of many of the world's most infamous/notorious criminals.
In this Unit the sentences should, where possible, be in the Passive and the expressions of dismay or disbelief should include some of those learnt in the Unit.

Structures: Exercises   Reading/Writing **A/B**

Exercise 1

1 was stolen / taken
2 are fastened / secured / locked / barred
3 are interested
4 was said to have / was reported to have
5 was picked ... broken / smashed
6 were searched
7 should (always) be kept / deposited / put
8 Has ... been paid.
9 being stolen / taken

10 were (you) interrogated / questioned by
11 are (not often) broken open.
12 was considered / thought to be
13 was given
14 was used to hit / kill
15 Have ... been caught
16 was being taken
17 had (never) been searched / stopped
18 were covered / stained
19 have to be paid
20 was ... abolished

Exercise 2

1 was arrested
2 were instructed
3 would be caught
4 is thought
5 was revved up

6 be controlled
7 cannot / must not be put
8 been given up
9 had been burgled
10 will be / has been let off

Exercise 3

The following are suggestions for completion of the sentences. Variations will occur to student and teacher.

1 were held up
2 must have been stolen
3 was allowed to sit down
4 was not considered reliable
5 had been punctured

6 be introduced to prevent mugging?
7 will be seriously delayed
8 must have been forced
9 are being searched
10 were stolen last month.

Exercise 4

1 has had a burglar alarm fitted
2 will have had the statements checked
3 had had the room cleaned
4 has had it repainted
5 had her wallet stolen
6 have had the ladder mended
7 has / must have had it dyed
8 can't have / hasn't had it washed today
9 had my baby vaccinated
10 will have him arrested

Exercise 5

1 needs mending / repairing
2 have had it mended / repaired
3 had it cut?
4 must have them checked / will have to have them checked
5 had him killed / shot / murdered
6 need re-typing
7 have had it surveyed
8 need answering / have to be answered
9 have it searched / examined
10 needs oiling

Exercise 6

1 be detected   2 laid   3 been employed   4 were paid   5 cut   6 serviced
7 doing / to be done   8 done   9 caring for   10 to be considered   11 gratified
12 be removed   13 would be left   14 to be killed   15 were done / was done
16 have been discovered   17 been broken   18 had been put / was put
19 was murdered / had been murdered   20 caught

Exercise 7

When so-called intelligent people commit crimes, they never imagine that the police will suspect them. They believe that if they make their plans with proper care, nothing can possibly go wrong. Their arrogance in fact usually causes their downfall. 'No one else has ever committed such a perfect crime,' they tell themselves, 'I've thought of every detail, others may make foolish mistakes, but I shan't make any – I am too clever!'

They are often too clever. They forget that the perfect crime fascinates people more than the obvious one. This in turn means that the police may investigate it more fully. His neighbours or workmates do not consider a man with a perfect alibi to be a likely suspect, but the law may regard him as rather too innocent. Ordinary people often confuse times and dates, particularly in moments of stress. Unless we keep an exact record, we easily forget what we were doing or where we were a month ago. What special reason is there for us to remember it? Our 'clever' criminal, on the other hand, makes sure that he can answer any question about time or place satisfactorily. He forgets that the police expect people to be nervous and uncertain when they interrogate them. In planning the perfect crime the criminal takes care to remember details that no one else would remember in similar circumstances, and this in itself may be the very reason why people cleverer than himself doubt his testimony.

Information Retrieval   Reading/Writing

1   ... Celeste killed Amy. She would not have been strong enough; it does not seem that she had a motive.
2   ... it is not likely that Louis Spanker killed her. If he had been into the room he would have taken the jewellery.
3   ... Joe killed her. He loved Amy, and she seems to have loved him, as she accepted flowers from him, and kept his portrait on her dressing table.
4   Henry Willy. He had a motive; he was jealous because Amy obviously preferred Joe to him; she had Joe's portrait and Joe had recently sent her flowers; when sitting at her dressing table Amy could see someone enter her room, and as there are no signs of a struggle it must have been someone she knew.

How to write a Description Reading/Writing   **D**
Exercise 2
1 C 2 B 3 D 4 C 5 A

Ask and Answer Reading/Writing   **E**
Are dogs hard to train? Yes, they are.
Should dog handlers have a special understanding of their dogs?
… it has a lot of exercise.
Why are dogs used to catch criminals? Because they have a very keen sense of
smell and can follows scents easily / Because they can be trained to attack
criminals and stop them escaping.
… they can see well in the dark and they can move quietly without being seen.
What effect does a notice saying 'guard dogs on the premises' have on the
public?
… it barks if anyone tries to enter the house and therefore scares burglars
away.
Why is an escaped prisoner afraid of police dogs being used? Because he
thinks the dog will track him down easily.

How to tell a Story Reading/Writing   **F**
Exercise 1

1	carefully / attentively / closely	6	seized / caught
2	moved slowly / cautiously / quietly	7	shouted
3	dry sound	8	stuttered / said hesitantly
4	ran quickly / very fast	9	burst out / said angrily
5	jumped / leapt / rushed	10	confounded / awful / uncontrolled

Exercise 3
1 To describe how the heat had dried the ground.
2 'Night fell like a heavy blanket, suffocatingly hot'.
3 'Stench' is an extremely unpleasant smell. It cannot be used for anything that
smells agreeable.
4 Mean and dishonest.
5 Because of the noise he made on his home-made guitar.
6 Water was rationed and had to be shared.
The men suffered from insect bites.
There was a constant smell of unwashed bodies.
7 It provided the only shade in the prison yard.
8 He had made a private arrangement with the guard.
9 Twang is said to be 'slow-witted', yet in these circumstances he is the one
who makes the first violent move. He shows courage. It is ironic that he is
among the first to die.
10 He escaped over the wall at the back of the cook-house while the fighting was
going on.

Unit seven: News and information

Drills and Exercises Oral   **B**
Exercise 1
No, he said it would be hot and humid.
No, he said they would die out by the early evening.
He said it would rise to about 30 degrees centigrade.

Exercise 2

Simon Shaw said there were roadworks on the A99 just outside Holchester and this / that / it was causing considerable delay. He also said there was a burst gas main in Holchester High Street and traffic was building up there, and they'd just had news of an accident in Seabourne at the junction of Beach Road and Carter's Lane. It seemed to be a pretty serious one so traffic was being diverted to Cook's Road. He said there was a heavy tail-back and the police said that anyone who could avoid this route would be well advised to do so / the police advised everyone to avoid this route if possible.

Note   Some variation of the actual words is permissible here.

Exercise 3

1   Mary thought Joan had said Radio Essex / Mary thought Joan had said she'd just been listening to Radio Essex.
2   Because she thought Joan said 'funny Tommy' instead of 'funny tummy' / Because she misunderstood what Joan said.
3   Joan said the commercial was about 'On-Tops'.
4   Mary said she was listening.
5   Mary thought the man had said you ought to stop when you got that sinking feeling.
6   Joan said he didn't say 'stop', he said 'Take On-Tops' and he'd told everyone to take 'On-Tops' if they wanted to be on top.
7   Mary asked Joan to speak more clearly because she was giving her a nervous headache.
8   Joan advised Mary to take 'On-Tops'.
9   Joan said she would ring her again later.
10   Joan wondered where her bottle of 'On-Tops' was.

Exercise 4

1   (a)   The Newsreader said the Chancellor of the Exchequer had announced cuts amounting to six hundred million pounds in an effort to stabilise Britain's economy in the coming year.
    (b)   The Newsreader said the Opposition had expressed outrage and disgust at these proposals and had called on the Chancellor to resign.
    (c)   The Newsreader said the price of petrol was to go up by 2p a gallon from September 1st.
2   The Newsreader said that the two eleven-year-old schoolboys who had been missing from their London homes for six weeks had been found in a youth hostel in the Lake District. He said they had been posing as French schoolboys visiting Britain but that their identity had been discovered when a party of genuine French boys had arrived at the hostel.

Exercise 5

1   (a)   He asked if I used *Sea Air*.
    (b)   He asked if I had to open the windows.
    (c)   He asked if Mary used cheap perfume.
    (d)   He asked if people noticed the cooking smells.
    (e)   He asked if Aunt Edith had bought chest liniment.
    (f)   He asked if my house was full of sea breezes.

2   (a)   He told us to use *Sea Air*.
    (b)   He told us to fill the house with sea breezes.
    (c)   He told us to give our house the right smell.
    (d)   He told us to try the handy bathroom size.
    (e)   He told us to buy the giant economy spray.
    (f)   He told us to puff once and breathe *Sea Air*.

In this exercise the student is required to give his own free report of what he heard.

Exercise 6

I said I'd been asked to give a talk on the radio.
I heard the Prime Minister say on the radio that he was increasing Family Allowances.
I read a report of an interview with a famous scientist in which he said he believed there might be life on Venus.
I asked if you would mind moving those parcels so that I could sit down.
What did you say the time was?

The above are suggested answers. Variations are permissible.

Reading Aloud   Oral   C

Because of industrial action (i.e. a strike) at Gatwick Airport.
Until further notice.
They will try to put passengers on to flights with other airlines.
They should contact their travel agency or phone Continental Airways.

Look and Say   Oral   D

He is speaking into the receiver. He is speaking on the telephone.
He is making a call / phoning a friend / his company, etc.
Pick up the receiver, dial the number, when you hear the pips insert a coin and speak.
Look it up in the telephone directory. If it's not there, ask the operator.
Not if the overseas number is on the direct dialling system, but if not you must ask the international operator to get the number for you.

Making a Telephone Call   Oral   E

Exercise 1

Can / May I speak to the Managing Director, please?
Is that the Managing Director?
Oh, then I'd like to speak to Mr Brown, please
Oh, then can / may I speak to Mr Brown, please?
Can / would you put me through to the Sales Manager's office, please?
All right, I'll hold on.
Can / May I leave a message?
I'll ring again later.

Variations are permissible.

Exercise 2

I'm afraid / I'm sorry he's out.
I'll put you through.
I'm afraid / I'm sorry his line's engaged.
Hold on a moment, I'll get him.
Would you like to leave a message? / Can I take a message?
I think he'll be back later / He'll be back about – o'clock.
I think you must have got the wrong number / I'm afraid you've got the wrong number.

Exercise 3

In this exercise the student is required to give a free report of the Nurse's message about Mrs Parkins' daughter.

Exercise 1

1   The producer said they wouldn't be able to record that afternoon.
2   He / she / I said he / she / I had seen him the previous morning.
3   He / The Manager asked Miss Brown if she could start the following month
4   The director warned us / them not to start speaking until the red light came
5   I asked him / her why he / she had done it when I had told him / her not to.
6   The producer exclaimed that he would never employ that actor again as he didn't project at all.
7   He / she / I asked Tom if he could speak up as he / she / I couldn't hear a word he was saying.
8   The boss said he / she / I ought not to take more than an hour for lunch.
9   He said he wished he could play 'Hamlet' in the new radio production.
10   She said that she was delighted that I / he / she had come to the studio, but wanted to know / wondered / asked why I / he / she hadn't come at ten o'clock.

Exercise 2

1   I telephoned at ten o'clock, but nobody answered.
2   I'll help you if I can, but it's difficult.
3   'Can you work late this evening?' the producer asked his secretary.
4   'I'm sorry I'm late,' said the actor, 'I was held up in a traffic jam.'
5   'If it rains, the cricket match will be postponed,' said the presenter.
6   'You're being difficult,' he said to them / he told them.
7   'Wait until the red light comes on,' the producer said to / told the actors.
8   'Who did you go to lunch with Bill?' asked Tom.
9   'The show is running over time,' he told us / informed us, 'can you speed up
10   'Oh dear, it's started raining and I haven't brought a raincoat,' she said.

Exercise 3

1   He warned me / him / her to mind / be careful of the microphone and not to break it.
    He warned me / him / her to be careful not to break the microphone.
2   He / she asked where his / her script was. He / She thought he / she had put it on the desk but it wasn't there now.
3   The producer sighed and remarked that the first recording was very bad.
4   I / he / she asked if he / she could tell me the way to Radio Wessex.
5   He / she told me / him / her to take the first turning on the left and then keep straight on.
6   He / she said he / she had never used Sea Air before, but he / she was going to try it after having heard our / my programme.
7   The teacher told us that the following day / the next day we would start on the new foreign language series.
8   I wonder if the new secretary's married.
    I / he / she wondered if the new secretary was married.
9   He / she / I wanted to know what he / she / they was / were doing.
10   He / she wished me good morning and complained what a terrible day it was

Exercise 4

1   'It's very annoying / It's a nuisance (etc.),' the technician complained, 'I often have to record the programme several times.'
2   'What time is it?' the reporter asked the typist.
3   'Hello, I'm sorry to tell you the last bus has just gone,' he said sadly.
4   'Don't call me before seven tomorrow morning,' the director said / instructed the switchboard operator.

5 'Can / Could / May / Might I use your phone?' she asked me.
6 'The programme will start in one minute,' said the presenter.
7 'Why aren't you playing / didn't you play / don't you play the leading role in the sketch?' I asked him.
8 'Ugh!' said Mrs Brown, 'I hate fish and chips.'
9 'I don't mind having lunch in the pub,' said the producer.
10 'I wonder if I'll get overtime,' said the actor.

Variations on the above are permissible, provided the sense of the sentence is retained.

Exercise 5

The travel agent told me that my plane left at 10.35 and that I had to be at the airport at 10 o'clock or, if I was coming from London, I could take the Irish Airways bus from the Kerry Hotel in Bayswater. That left at 9.30, so I would have to be at the Kerry Hotel, by, say, 9.15. He said that the plane arrived in Dublin at 11.30 a.m. and then I could take the airport bus to the Dublin bus centre. He said they went every twenty minutes, and the Killarney Hotel was about five minutes' walk from the bus centre. When I asked, he told me the return bus fare was included in the price of my ticket.

Variations permissible

Exercise 6

Self	Oh, Mrs Gordon, I have to be away for a few days. Would you mind looking after my cat and watering my plants?
Mrs Gordon	I'd be glad to.
Self	By the way, the cat only eats raw liver or fried haddock.
Mrs Gordon	Ugh! I don't like the sight of raw liver, it makes me feel ill, and as for frying haddock, I can't stand the smell!
Self	Well, it's not you who are going to eat the liver, and there's no need to look at it if you don't want to.
Mrs Gordon	Oh, I really don't know / I'm not at all sure …
Self	As for the fried haddock, I always get that ready cooked from the fish and chip shop at the corner. The cat's very fond of it and it often comes with me and waits outside till I come out of the shop.
Mrs Gordon	It's ridiculous / absurd / disgusting (etc.) The fools people make of themselves over animals.
Self	Oh, and you won't forget about watering the plants, will you?
Mrs Gordon	Where are they?
Self	They're in a window box on the window sill upstairs. They need to be watered twice a day. They won't be any trouble.
Mrs Gordon	How do you think I'm going to be able to reach them without a ladder?
Self	Really, I don't think it's asking too much to feed a neighbour's cat and water her plants while she's away.
Mrs Gordon	Indeed! Well, it's not a case of what you think but what you expect other people to do. Why don't you ask someone else? / You'd better ask someone else!

Variations permissible

Exercise 7

In an interview on radio, Freddie, the famous athlete who has just announced his retirement, was asked how it felt to be the strongest man in the world. He said that it felt great but that in a way it was a kind of vindication. When asked what he meant by this, he explained that when he was / had been a child, he was always / had always been skinny and weak and was always being / had always been

teased about it at school. In the end, he said, the only thing he (had) wanted to do
was to prove that he was bigger and stronger than anyone. It had become a kind
of obsession, he supposed. Asked what his plans were now, Freddie said that he
was retiring. He wanted to spend some time with his family and he thought he
had earned it.

Variations permissible

Exercise 8

Chairman The Historic Buildings Association will strongly resist the local
Council's proposal to demolish Chumstead Hall, the home of the
eighteenth century poet, Walter Bury, in order to erect a new
secondary school on the site. A petition is now being organised and
there are plans for a protest demonstration outside the House of
Commons.

Ask and Answer   Reading/Writing C

1 What kind of container is this? It's a spray can / canister / pressurised
   container.
2 ... it smells of the sea / ozone.
3 Why is this type of product sometimes dangerous? Because the vapour can be
   inhaled / Because it is inflammable / Because the container may explode when
   heated.
4 ... on television ... most people watch it / it has a large audience.
5 Why would this particular product appeal to women?
6 ... it is difficult to dispose of / shouldn't be burnt / can't be destroyed.
7 Where would you use *Sea Air*? I'd use it in the kitchen / bathroom.
8 How could *Sea Air* improve your home?
9 Why is advertising so expensive? A lot of people are involved in making an
   advert. Air / viewing time is expensive to buy. Space in newspapers or
   magazines is expensive to buy.
10 Free answer. Suggestion: *Wave-Fresh*.

How to write Reports, Talks and
Speeches   Reading/Writing D

Exercise 1, 2 and 3

Free composition required from the student, based on the forms already discussed
in the Unit.

Exercise 4

Several variations are possible. The main points are given below.

1 ... nitrogen has been found; it is essential to life; even a minute quantity
   might mean there is or was life.
2 ... he says what he thinks people want to hear; he talks in a pompous voice so
   people think he has a great mind; it seems as though he has the confidence of
   scientists.
3 ... even scientists are uncertain about life on Venus; it could take weeks before
   anyone could be sure, but he thinks the indications are positive.
4 ... is low because Christopher Miles says what people want to hear; he's not a
   scientist; he strings together bits and pieces of information; he makes himself
   sound important; he doesn't make original predictions of his own.

Reading Comprehension   Reading/Writing E
1 *C*   2 *B*   3 *B*   4 *C*   5 *B*

Drills and Exercises   Oral   **B**

Exercise 1

I'd rather you took that on.
Do get on with it.
Get back there, please!
I think he's coming round.
Don't try to get up.
She means she hopes no-one will find out she's never given the kiss of life before.
Bob thought the man didn't look as though he was going to get over the fall.

8 Because he felt hot / faint / dizzy / sick.

9 Take up nursing.

10 She'd come across an article in one of the Sunday papers.

11 He said it was the fourth bright idea she'd come up with in the last week.

12 He meant she never had time to do anything new.

Exercise 2

Then it's time you got round to it.
Then it's time he got on with it.
Then it's time she got over it.
Then it's time they got back.

5 Then it's time he got up.

6 Then it's time he got round to it.

7 Then it's time you got on with it.

8 Then it's time he got over it.

Exercise 3

No, it came out after the operation.
No, she came round after the operation.
No, they came across it after the operation.
No, it came up after the operation.
No, it came out after the operation.
No, she came round after the operation.
No, I came across it after the operation.
No, it came up after the operation.

Exercise 4

Why don't you take them off?
Why don't you take it up?
Why didn't he take to it?
Why did you take it on?

5 Why didn't she take to it?

6 Why don't you take it off?

7 Why doesn't she take it up?

8 Why didn't he take to it?

Describing Aches and Pains   Oral   **C**

Exercise 1

She's rubbing her ankle because she's sprained it.
She's wearing a bandage on her hand because she's scalded it.
She's sneezing because she's got a cold.
Her face is swollen because she's got toothache.
She has spots on her neck because she's got a rash.
She has a swelling on her arm because she's been stung by a bee.
She can't walk because her feet are numb.
Her head is going round because she feels dizzy.

Exercise 2

I've got a cold.
I've got a blister.
I've got a rash.

4 I've scalded it.

5 I've sprained it.

6 I've got toothache.

7 I've got a headache.

8 I've got a sore throat.

Exercise 3

When he had a cold, he sneezed.
When he had a blistered heel, he limped.

29

3 When he had a sore throat, he sounded hoarse.
4 When he had a rash, he scratched.
5 When he cut his finger, he bled.
6 When he spilt the hot water, he scalded himself.
7 When he sprained his wrist, he rubbed it.
8 When he felt dizzy, he fainted.

Look and Answer   Oral

1 There is an ambulance, specially for handicapped children, standing in the street outside a hospital.
2 Children with a physical defect, often with something wrong with their legs (arms, or body; but they could be blind or deaf.
3 It has special equipment and teaching for handicapped children.
4 Free answer.

Listening Comprehension   Oral
Text 1
Peter Baxter   5 Queen's Avenue, Highgate
25   Single
Smallpox vaccination   YES
Measles   YES
Diphtheria   YES
Typhoid   NO
Cholera   NO
Poliomyelitis   YES
Chest X-ray   YES, 1979
Tuberculosis   NO
Migraine   NO
Allergic to shellfish
Glasses: reading   YES
                watching TV   NO
                long distance   NO
Tested: November, 1983
a) hearing aid   NO
b) dentures   NO
Dentist: August 1981
Text 2
1 C   2 B   3 B   4 D   5 B

Reading Aloud   Oral
1 In an advertisement in a newspaper or magazine; on the packet.
2 To ease the discomfort of headache, toothache, rheumatic pain and the symptoms of 'flu, colds and sore throats.
3 Because it is soluble (it dissolves in liquid).
4 One if the child is between six and twelve years, none if it is under six.

Structures: Exercises   Reading/Writing   A/
Exercise 1
1 broke down	4 get about / around	7 get up
2 brought up	5 make up	8 set out
3 put (me) through	6 put out	9 take off

10	is (she) on / off	15	brought (her) round	18	put away
11	give up			19	took down
12	got over	16	taken out	20	turned down
13	put off	17	broke out		
14	get through … turn back				

Exercise 2

The following completions are suggestions; there are several variations possible, but the students should use a Phrasal Verb in each sentence.

1	break down	8	gets me down	15	get up
2	gets behind	9	get up	16	taken aback
3	threw up	10	gone into	17	turned away
4	bring her round	11	gone off	18	set her back
5	was called in	12	making things up	19	take off your clothes
6	came into	13	put it down to	20	get through it
7	got out	14	put up with		

Exercise 3

1	put off	8	took to	15	pulled out
2	put in for	9	make up	16	making for
3	put by	10	went over	17	not making it up
4	given up	11	taking on	18	take on
5	had turned out	12	took off	19	got away
6	didn't get on	13	come up	20	go through
7	turned up	14	put up with		

Exercises 4 and 5

Free composition based on the passage given.

Vocabulary: Photograph   Reading/Writing   C

1	skeleton	5	shoulders	9	fingers
2	skull	6	ribs / ribcage	10	knee (bone)
3	neck	7	elbow (joint)	11	ankle (bone)
4	spine / backbone	8	wrist (bone)	12	toes

Reading Comprehension   Reading/Writing   D

1 A 2 B 3 D 4 C 5 B 6 D 7 B 8 A 9 C 10 B 11 D 12 D
13 A 14 D 15 D 16 A 17 A 18 D 19 B 20 C 21 A 22 C 23 D
24 C 25 A 26 D 27 C 28 A 29 B 30 D 31 A 32 C 33 A 34 B
35 C 36 D 37 B 38 C 39 A 40 C

Reading Comprehension   Reading/Writing   E

1 C 2: B1, D2, A3, C4 3 A 4 C 5 B

Putting it Another Way   Reading/Writing   F

Exercise 1

1 'When does the post arrive?' he asked.
2 Two of his ribs were broken in the fight.
3 It was such a beautiful day we decided to have a picnic.
4 There was a photograph of his wife in his wallet.
5 He's too ill to come to the party tomorrow.
6 It is quite entertaining to watch the sports programmes on television.
7 Did Turner paint that picture?

8   That exercise is not difficult enough for my class.
9   The old man asked if I could tell him where the Post Office was.
10 John has more work than Stephen.
11 Teaching children to spell is hard work.
12 The apples were so cheap, I bought two pounds.
13 The fire broke out at half-past one.
14 I don't know as much about painting as my husband does.
15 'I never have time to go to the cinema,' she told me.
16 It took Philip about two years to translate that book.
17 His brother is shorter than he is.
18 I asked the children to leave me alone as I was very tired.
19 There was nothing interesting in the newspaper today.
20 It is about six miles from here to Canterbury / Canterbury is about six miles from here.
21 No one knows him as well as I do.
22 It was such an interesting book, I read it again.
23 'Be quiet, children,' said the teacher.
24 He asked me what my name was.
25 Sarah likes jazz more than I do.

Exercise 2

1   He can't possibly catch the 7.30 train.
2   Hasn't that tin got any sugar in it?
3   His house is not for sale.
4   He spoke very bad English.
5   How far is it from here to London?
6   Have you ever been to London before?
7   Which would you like, sausages or fish?
8   He is a very careless worker.
9   What did you pay for that dress?
10 I shall always stay at home.
11 Is there a swimming pool at the school?
12 It takes six hours to drive from here to Birmingham.

Word Building   Reading/Writing

Exercise 1
1 impolite   2 clarify   3 authorisation   4 true   5 Illiteracy   6 capable
7 difficult   8 fussiness   9 anger   10 unfortunately   11 careful   12 discretion
13 insane   14 impossibility   15 sleepiness   16 cheerful   17 signifies
18 undated   19 boyhood   20 plentiful

Exercise 2
1 medical   2 complaints   3 advertisements   4 knowledgeable   5 imaginary
6 treatment   7 troublesome   8 unable   9 valuable   10 illegal

Exercise 3
1 gratitude   2 contribution   3 carefulness   4 extravagant   5 enjoyment
6 excitement   7 horror   8 troublesome   9 fussy   10 awfulness

Exercise 4
1 attention   2 occupation   3 daily   4 belief   5 attractive   6 argument
7 intention   8 fortunately   9 payment   10 independence